Monster Countdown

by Pamela Jane
Illustrated by Nick Zarin-Ackerman

MONDO

For my niece, Camile—P.J.
To Mom, Dad, and Gerald—N.Z.A.

Text copyright © 2001 by Pamela Jane
Illustrations copyright © 2001 by Nick Zarin-Ackerman
under exclusive license to MONDO Publishing

For information contact:
MONDO Publishing
980 Avenue of the Americas
New York, NY 10018
Visit our web site at http://www.mondopub.com

Printed in the United States of America
01 02 03 04 05 06 07 HC 9 8 7 6 5 4 3 2 1
01 02 03 04 05 06 07 PB 9 8 7 6 5 4 3 2 1

ISBN 1-58653-857-8 (hardcover)   ISBN 1-59034-062-0 (paperback.)

Designed by Marina Maurici
Production by Danny Adlerman

Library of Congress Cataloging-in-Publication Data

Jane, Pamela.
    Monster countdown : a spooky counting book / by Pamela Jane ; illustrated by Nick Zarin-Ackerman.
        p. cm.
    Summary: In a rhyming countdown from ten to one, a boy describes the wacky
monsters all over his house.
    ISBN 1-58653-857-8
    [1. Monsters--Fiction. 2. Counting. 3. Stories in rhyme.] I. Zarin-Ackerman, Nick, ill.
II. Title.

PZ8.3.J158 Mm 2001
[E]--dc21
                                                            2001034304

My house is full of monsters.
They keep me on the run.
Ready for the countdown?
Let's go from ten to one!

10 monsters on the washer
Jump in with all the clothes.
They spin around until they're flat,
Then hang out by their toes!

9 monsters in the attic,
Behind my grandma's trunk.
Those monsters cannot budge an inch
Because of all the junk.

8 monsters sliding down the walls,
Dark shadows in the night.
If they dare come any closer
I'll just turn on the light!

7 monsters in the trash can!
I hear a gleeful shout—
"We love to stomp and play in here,
But please don't throw us OUT!"

6 monsters in the hallway,
Hanging on the hooks.
I'd march right up and say, "Hello!"
But I don't like their looks.

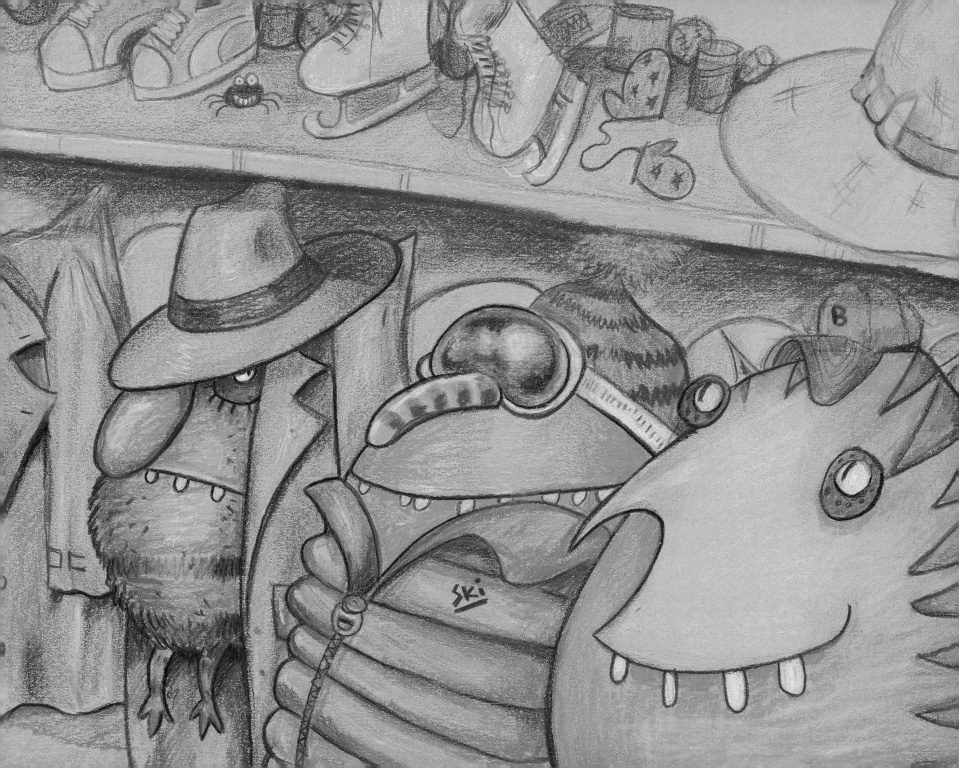

5 monsters sneaking up the stairs!
I hear the old floor creak.
I tiptoe up behind them—
But they don't see me peek!

4 monsters snacking in my room
On crayons, chalk, and stuff.
Munching, crunching all night long,
They never get enough!

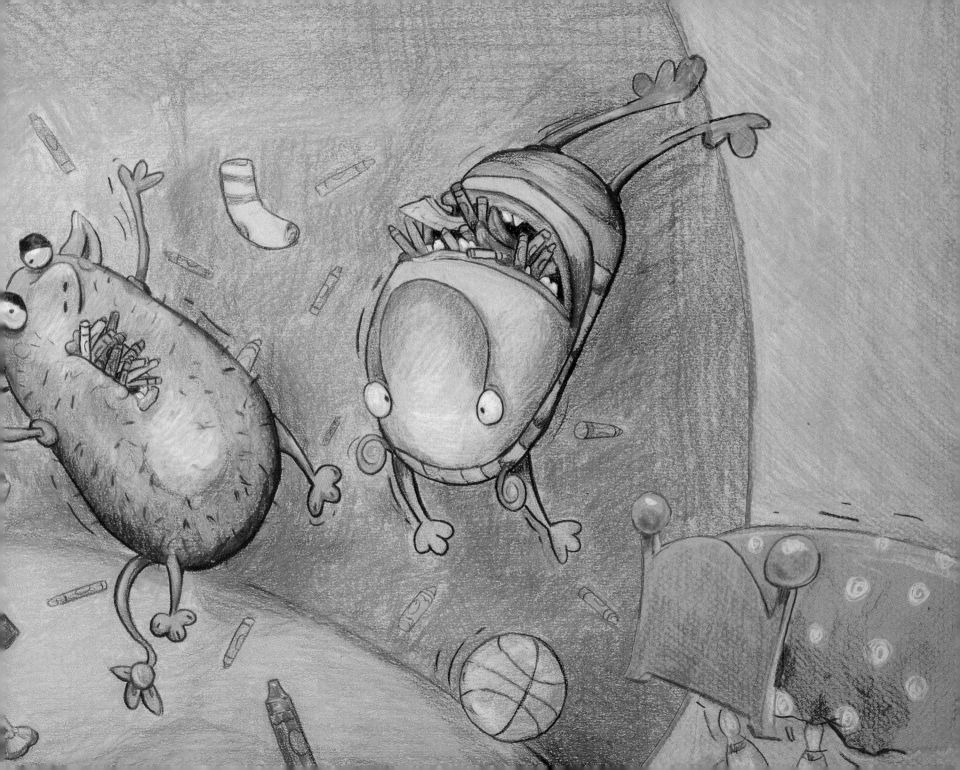

3 monsters on the drainpipe,
Beneath the bathroom sink.
Those thirsty monsters gurgle
Each time I take a drink.

2 monsters in my closet.
They play behind my clothes.
I chase them and then—"Gotcha!"
I grab them by the nose.

1 very funny monster
I know I'll always see—
The monster in the mirror
Making faces back at me!

I never ever fear the dark,
Not even for a minute—
Because I know I'm not alone
With all my monsters in it!